Les Aventures de Pierre

...autour du monde francophone

Written by Ryan Bolduc & Taylor Moorehead

Illustrated by Callum Bullers

Creo En Ti

Salut, mes amis! Je m'appelle Pierre, et je suis en train de faire mes valises pour mon voyage autour du monde francophone. C'est un excellent moyen de découvrir d'autres cultures et de rencontrer de nouveaux gens en cours de route. Voudriez-vous venir avec moi?

Hello, my friends! My name is Pierre, and I am packing my bags for my trip around the French-speaking world. It's an excellent way to learn about other cultures and meet new people along the way. Would you like to join me on my journey?

Le premier arrêt de notre voyage est dans mon pays natal, **la France!** Par là- bas, il y a **la tour Eiffel, le Louvre, et la Notre Dame.** A 324 m de hauteur, **la tour Eiffel** est le plus grand monument de France. **Le Louvre** est le plus grand musée au monde, avec 380,000 œuvres d'art, la plus fameuse de celles étant la Joconde. **La Notre Dame** a commencé d'être construite en 1163, et il était fini presque 200 années plus tard en 1345.

The first stop on our trip is my home country, **France!** Over there is **the Eiffel Tower, the Louvre**, and **the Notre Dame.** At 1,063 feet, **the Eiffel Tower** is the tallest building in France. **The Louvre** is the biggest museum in the world, with 380,000 works of art, the most famous of them is the Mona Lisa. **The Notre Dame** started being built in 1163, and it was finished almost 200 years later in 1345.

Allons-y, nous allons rater notre taxi pour la gare!

Let's go, we are going to miss our taxi to the train station!

Voici la Belgique! C'est un pays voisin de la France. La Belgique propose de nombreux aliments différents tels que **les frites** et **les gaufres belges**. Les belges aiment ces différents aliments presque autant qu'ils aiment leurs équipes de foot. L'équipe de foot belge est classée parmi les **dix meilleures au monde**! Si vous pouvez visiter la Belgique, vous trouverez de nombreux **saxophones**, car **Adolphe Sax** y a inventé l'instrument en 1846.

Here is Belgium! It's a neighboring country to France. Belgium is home to many unique foods such as **french fries** and **Belgian waffles**. Belgians love their food almost as much as they love soccer. The Belgian soccer team is ranked in the **top ten in the world**! If you visit Belgium, you will find many **saxophones** because **Adolphe Sax** invented the instrument here in 1846.

Ne sois pas en retard, la Côte D'ivoire n'attend pas!

Don't be late, the Ivory Coast doesn't wait!

La température plus chaude signifie que **nous sommes arrivés en Côte d'Ivoire!** La Côte d'Ivoire est un petit pays localisé dans la côté ouest de l'Afrique. **33% des fèves de cacao** au monde sont produites ici, et ces fèves sont utilisées pour faire le chocolat. De plus, la Côte d'Ivoire abrite **la plus grande église au monde**, d'une taille d'environ 4 terrains de foot réunis!

The hot temperatures mean that **we've arrived on the Ivory Coast**. The Ivory Coast is a small country located on the west coast of Africa. **33% of the world's cacao beans** are produced here, and these beans are used to make chocolate. In addition, the Ivory Coast is home to **the largest church on earth**, which is almost big as 4 soccer fields put together.

Je vous verrai **quand nous arriverons à Madagascar!**

See you **once we arrive in Madagascar!**

Allô, de Madagascar! Cette île est **la quatrième plus grande** au monde! Il abrite **plus de 50%** de **la population mondiale des caméléons**, qui peuvent changer de couleur afin de se camouflager dans l'environnent. Madagascar abrite également **70 espèces de lémuriens** qui sont uniques à l'île, que l'on ne peut trouver nulle part ailleurs au monde!

Hey from Madagascar! This island is the **fourth largest island** in the world! It is home to **more than 50%** of the **chameleon population** in the world, and they can change colors to blend in with the environment. Madagascar is also home to **70 species of lemurs** that you can't find anywhere else in the world!

Prends ton maillot de bain. Nous allons nager!

Grab your swimsuits. We are going for a swim!

Voilà les Seychelles! Ces îles sont connues pour leurs plages de sable blanc et leur eau crystalline bleue. Une île, qui s'appelle **l'île d'oiseau**, abrite de la plus grande tortue dans le monde, **Esmeralda**! En fait, il pèse plus de **300 kilogrammes**! Il y a plus de tortues que de gens aux Seychelles. Les îles consistent en granite, et les Seychelles sont les seules îles faites complètement en granite.

This is the Seychelles! The islands are known for their white sand beaches and their crystal clear water. One island, named **Bird Island**, is the home of the biggest tortoise in the world, **Esmerelda**! He weighs more than **650 pounds**! There are more tortoises than people in Seychelles. The islands are made of granite, and the Seychelles are the only islands made completely of granite.

Maintenant, montons à bord de notre bateau de croisière
et **partons pour la Polynésie française!**

Now, let's hop on our cruise ship and **head to French Polynesia!**

Dites bonjour à la Polynésie française! Le pays est constitué de **118 îles**—c'est beaucoup! Sur l'île, il y a des maisons construites au-dessus de l'océan. Les personnes d'îles ne reçoivent pas leur courrier dans leurs boîtes aux lettres plutôt ils reçoivent **du pain** et ils doivent aller à la poste pour obtenir leur courrier.

Say hello to French Polynesia! The country is made up of **118 islands**—that's a lot! On the island, there are homes built above the water. The people of the islands don't receive their mail in their mailboxes, instead, they receive **bread** and they must go to the post office to get their mail.

Mettons les manteaux, parce que nous irons vers le nord, au Canada!

Bundle up, because we're going up north to **Canada!**

Nous venons d'arriver au Canada!
Le Canada est le **deuxième plus grand pays** au monde. Il abrite plus de la moitié de la population mondiale **d'ours polaires**. L'un des plats canadiens les plus connus est la **poutine**, des frites garnies de fromage et de sauce. C'est délicieux!

We've just arrived in Canada! Canada is the **second-largest country** in the world! It is home to more than half of the world's population of **polar bears**! One of the most well-known Canadian dishes is **poutine**, fries topped with cheese and gravy. It's delicious!

N'oubliez pas d'apporter beaucoup de crème solaire *pour notre prochaine destination!*

Don't forget to bring some sunscreen *to our next destination!*

Je présente la Haïti! Ce pays a beaucoup de montagnes, et en fait, le nom Haïti signifie **"le pays montagneux"**. Chaque année, les personnes haïtiens célèbrent la fête, **le Carnival**. Beaucoup d'autres pays célèbrent le Carnival aussi!

I present Haiti! This country has a lot of mountains, in fact, the name Haiti means **"the mountainous country"**. Every year, the people of Haiti celebrate the holiday, **Carnival**. Many other francophone countries celebrate Carnival as well.

Montez dans le hélicoptère, nous partons pour notre destination finale, la Guyane française!

Hop in the helicopter, we're departing for our final destination, French Guiana!

Nous avons atterri au Centre Spatial de Guyane! Ici, ils lancent **beaucoup de fusées spatiales en l'espace**! Si tu as faim, nous pouvons arrêter à Cayenne, la capitale, ou **le poivre de Cayenne** est né.

We have landed at the Guiana Space Centre! Here, they launch **many rocket ships into space!** If you are hungry we can stop in Cayenne, the capital, where the **Cayenne pepper** originated.

On peut voir l'océan d'ici! La plage de la Guyane française abrite des tortues-luths, et ces plages sont un des **plus grands sites de nidification pour les tortues-luths**.

You can see the ocean from here! The beaches of French Guiana are home to leatherback turtles, and the beaches are **some of the largest nesting sites for leatherback turtles!**

Je me suis bien amusé voyager avec vous, mais c'est l'heure de retourner **en France!**

I had a great time traveling with you, but it's time to return **to France!**

Merci de me rejoindre tout au long de mon voyage dans le monde francophone! J'espère que tu l'as aimé autant que moi! **Quelle partie a été ton favori?** Le mien a bien été certainement quand nous avons vu les **caméléons à Madagascar**, ou bien quand nous avons mangé de la **poutine au Canada**, ou bien quand nous avons vu les **vaisseaux spatiaux en Guyane française**! Pendant notre voyage ensemble, nous avons pu apprendre beaucoup de choses sur les pays francophones et les cultures qui nous différencient!

Thanks for joining me on my adventure around the francophone world, I hope you enjoyed it as much as I did! **What was your favorite part?** Mine was definitely when we saw the **chameleons in Madagascar**, or when we ate **poutine in Canada**, or maybe when we saw the **spaceships in French Guiana**! During our time together, we learned so many new things about francophone countries and the cultures that make them unique!

Je souhaite que tu me rejoignes pour mon prochain voyage!

I hope you will join me on my next adventure!

Suivez les aventures de Pierre !
Follow Pierre's Adventures!

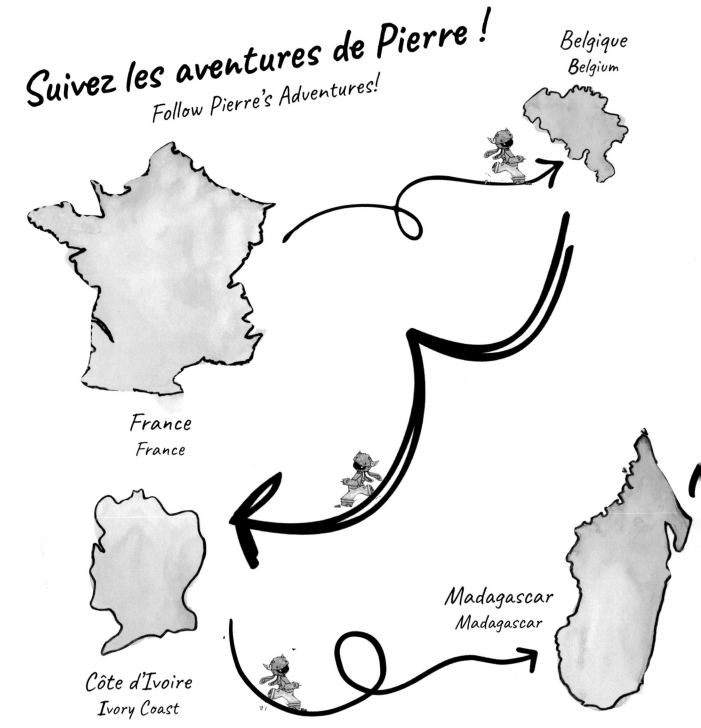

Belgique
Belgium

France
France

Côte d'Ivoire
Ivory Coast

Madagascar
Madagascar

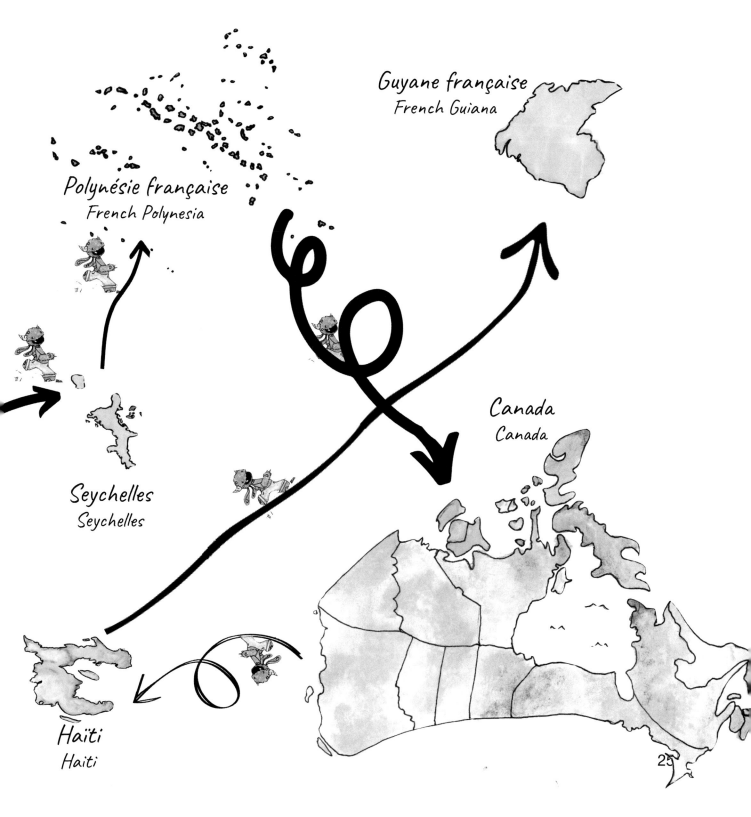

Guyane française
French Guiana

Polynésie française
French Polynesia

Seychelles
Seychelles

Canada
Canada

Haïti
Haiti

25

To my parents, Jim and Anne Bolduc
-Ryan

To my parents, Timothy Moorehead Jr. and Iesha Queen Moorehead
-Taylor

To my parents, Tom Bullers and Cherie Marvel
-Callum

and

To all of our French teachers who helped us along the way, Mrs. McDonough, Mr. Ridgeway, Ms. Christophe, Mrs. Miller, and Ms. Leonard

Creo En Ti Media

www.creoentimedia.com

Text Copyright © 2022 Ryan Bolduc & Taylor Moorehead

Images Copyright © 2022 Callum Bullers

ISBN-13: 978-1-949929-81-2 (paperback)

Library of Congress Control Number- In production

Creo En Ti

Authors & Illustrator

Ryan is a high school senior at McDonogh School in Maryland and has been studying French for more than 14 years. Ryan pursued many different extracurricular activities in high school, including the publication of Pierre's Adventure Around the Francophone World. In college, Ryan plans to pursue a double major in international relations and French and hopes to continue writing and publishing.

Taylor is a high school senior and is involved in a plethora of extracurricular activities, most notably the collaborative creation of *Pierre's Adventures Around the Francophone World*. Throughout her academic career, Taylor studied the French language for six consecutive years, and has started to pursue creative writing. Next year, she will attend Duke University at which she will study at the Trinity College of Arts & Sciences and hopes to continue publishing her work in the years to come.

Callum is an eighth grade student in Maryland who started drawing at a very young age, and completed his first sketchbook before kindergarten. Callum began learning French in fifth grade, and discovered his love of the French language. Callum plans to continue to create art

Ryan Bolduc,
Author

Taylor Moorehead,
Author

Callum Bullers,
Illustrator

About Creo En Ti Media

Creo En Ti is a Spanish phrase which means "I believe in you." Creo En Ti Media began in Lisa Pietropola's AP Spanish class at Northern High School in South Central Pennsylvania as a student-centered, bilingual literacy project designed to promote early childhood literacy. It developed into a cross-curricular endeavor combining art and foreign language content areas. This project created an opportunity for outstanding student work to be published and available to children and educators. Creo En Ti Media strives to give parents and educators the tools to spark an interest in language learning at a young age.

For more information about this project, including lesson plans for Spanish language classes, ESL classes and activities for parents and early childhood educators, please visit our website at www.creoentimedia.com

"Creo en ti means so much more than simply 'I believe in you.' It is the pillar of my teaching philosophy. Educators, like parents, pour their hearts and souls into the growth and success of their children. Students need to be filled with a sense of security before learning can take place. That is where Creo en ti comes in."
  –Lisa Pietropola

Creo En Ti

www.creoentimedia.com

Our Creative Director

Lisa Pietropola is the Creative Director of Creo En Ti Media and has spent 15 years in both the public and private school systems advocating for world languages. Lisa has built her career on establishing confidence in her students and using that confidence to empower lives. The recipient of the Outstanding Teacher of the Year Award, 2017, Lisa holds a Master of Arts degree in Spanish from Saint Louis University, Madrid, Spain. Lisa's years living abroad molded her approach to language learning. She continues to teach and inspire students today and is certified in both Spanish and English as a Second Language. Along with leading educational trips abroad, Lisa enjoys traveling with her husband and their two daughters.

"I am most proud of this endeavor not only because of the empowerment of second language learning, but also because we are raising a generation of students who have educators who believe in them."
–Lisa Pietropola

Made in the USA
Middletown, DE
12 July 2022